GW00482001

Gallery Books
Editor: Peter Fallon

WORDS IN THE AIR

Derek Mahon

WORDS IN THE AIR

A selection of poems by
Philippe Jaccottet
with translations and
an introduction by
Derek Mahon

Gallery Books

Words in the Air
is first published
simultaneously in paperback
and in a clothbound edition
in November 1998.

The Gallery Press
Loughcrew
Oldcastle
County Meath
Ireland

*All rights reserved. For permission
to reprint or broadcast these translations
write to The Gallery Press.*

Poems © Philippe Jaccottet/Éditions Gallimard
1953, 1957, 1967, 1969, 1977, 1983
Translations © Derek Mahon 1987, 1998

ISBN 1 85235 238 8 (*paperback*)
    1 85235 239 6 (*clothbound*)

The Gallery Press acknowledges the financial assistance
of An Chomhairle Ealaíon / The Arts Council, Ireland,
and the Arts Council of Northern Ireland.

Contents

Introduction *page* 11

'*La nuit est une grande cité endormie*' 16
'The June night is like a city of the dead' 17
'*Comme je suis un étranger dans notre vie*' 18
'Being a stranger in this life, I speak' 19
'*Je sais maintenant que je ne possède rien*' 20
'I know now I possess nothing of my own' 21
Portovenere 22
Portovenere 23
Intérieur 24
Interior 25
Les eaux et les forêts 26
Streams and Forests 27
Au petit jour 30
Daybreak 31
La patience 32
Patience 33
La voix 34
The Voice 35
L'ignorant 36
Ignorance 37
Les gitans 38
The Gipsies 39
Sur les pas de la lune 40
In the Steps of the Moon 41
Paroles dans l'air 42
Words in the Air 43
Le locataire 44
The Tenant 45
Que la fin nous illumine 46
That the End Enlighten Us 47
Dans un tourbillon de neige 48
During a Snowstorm 49
Les distances 50
Distances 51

Fin d'hiver 52
'Une semaison de larmes' 52
End of Winter 53
'A dispersion of tears' 53
Dans l'herbe à l'hiver survivant 54
Lune à l'aube d'été 54
'These wood-shadows, timid, patient' 55
Dawn Moon 55
Dans l'enceinte du bois d'hiver 56
Toute fleur n'est que de la nuit 56
'Without entering you can seize' 57
'Each flower is a little night' 57
Martinets 58
Il y aura toujours dans mon oeil cependant 58
Monde né d'une déchirure 58
Swifts 59
'Meanwhile my eye will retain' 59
'World born of a lesion' 59
Raisins et figues 60
'Grapes and figs' 61
Entre la plus lointaine étoile et nous 62
'Between us and the farthest star' 63
S'il se pouvait (qui saura jamais rien?) 64
'If it should be, and who can ever be sure' 65
Chose brève, le temps de quelques pas dehors 66
'Nothing at all, a footfall on the road' 67
On voit 68
Glimpses 69
Le mot joie 72
The Word Joy 73
À Henry Purcell 74
To Henry Purcell 75

Acknowledgements 79

WORDS IN THE AIR

Introduction

Most people approach contemporary French verse with trepidation, suspecting (often rightly) that what they are being asked to read will prove to be puzzling, gratuitous, angular, abstract, inflated and doctrinaire, bearing little resemblance to poetry as it's understood in the rest of the world; but readers of Jaccottet need have no such fears. Unlike the closely interlocked cycles of Yves Bonnefoy, or the open-plan notations of André du Bouchet, Jaccottet's work is recognizably circumstantial, and empirical in its relation to 'reality'. Unlike many French poets, moreover, he is not greatly troubled by the disjunction between the signifying word and the thing signified; language is a given and suffices for his purpose, the lyrical apprehension of a given world.

He began as an urban poet, a poet of post-war Paris; *L'Effraie* ('The Screech Owl', 1953) is full of alienation, existential fear and the onus of self-definition. The first poem in the volume, and therefore in the collected works, speaks already of death and the extinction of stars. Within a few pages he has described himself as 'a stranger in this life' and declared that he 'possesses nothing'. There are love poems too; but it's not until *L'Ignorant* ('Ignorance', 1957), completed after his marriage and removal to Grignan (Drôme), that he starts to come into his own; and for many readers this remains his outstanding collection. Several of his most admired poems are there — the title poem, 'Patience', 'The Voice' and 'The Tenant'; but *L'Ignorant*, impressive though it is, was also a clearing of space for something else. Having declared himself an 'ignorant' man, without 'possessions', he was ready to make his first significant advance. *Airs* (1967) is concerned with beginnings: '*À partir de rien, là est ma loi; tout le reste, fumée lointaine*' ('To start from nothing, that's my rule; everything else, distant smoke.') There is something of Beckett about this, the Beckett who spoke, in the *Dialogues*, of 'an art unresentful of its insuperable indigence' and declared that 'to be an artist is to fail as no other dare fail, failure is his world and the shrink from it desertion'; but Jaccottet means to *start* from nothing, not to *end* there. He too speaks of '*le presque rien à dire*' ('the almost nothing to say'); but he finds Beckett too 'systematic' and, besides, Jaccottet is in love with the earth. Between flowery Grignan and Beckett's 'hole in the Marne mud' stretches a world of difference.

'Outside the cliques, unbothered with the fashion', in MacNeice's phrase, he has pursued a private vision consciously resistant to systematization. So much has been written as the demonstration of a theory, or in anticipation of certain kinds of critical exposition, rather than as primary artistic endeavour, that Jaccottet's resistance to the trend has acquired an exemplary, even a heroic quality. Like other minimalists he knows exiguity and exasperation; his '*Que reste-t-il?*' ('What remains?') places him in the tradition of solitary inquiry of which Diogenes, Montaigne and *L'Innommable* are but three examples: 'What remains to me is practically nothing; but it's like a narrow gate you have to go through'; and he proclaims his purpose as '*tirer de la limite même un chant*' ('to draw a song from the very limit').

A student of Rilke, he wishes to be '*attentif à ce qui, d'un autre monde, affleure dans le nôtre*' ('attentive to what, from another world, appears in our own') — the classic definition of a miracle; and he asks himself the Rilkean questions. Behind Jaccottet lie lines from the *Duino Elegies* like 'the uninterrupted news that grows out of silence' and 'here is the time of the tellable, here is its home' (tr. J. B. Leishman) — though, in fairness to Jaccottet, he avoids '*la tentation de s'isoler en oraison, ce qui gêne quelque-fois chez Rilke'* ('the temptation to lose oneself in prayer, so irritating at times in Rilke'). One of the great poets of daybreak, in his role of 'first comer', early riser, he attends to 'the neglected things':

> *At the end of the shadiest paths,*
> *among the brambles, you will find an anemone*
> *bright and ordinary like the morning star.*

He is a secular mystic. 'The natural object is always the adequate symbol,' said Pound; and Jaccottet's symbols are the elemental, pre-Socratic ones: tree, flower, sun, moon, road, hill, wind, water, bird, house, lamp. He is fascinated by light, especially what John le Carré calls 'the religious light between dawn and morning'; and by lamplit twilight, *l'heure bleue*, the complex dusk of Magritte's *L'empire des lumières*. His characteristic posture is that of a man alone in a garden watching the sun rise, *'rebaptisé chaque matin par le jour'* ('re-baptised each morning by daybreak'), or seated at his desk by lamplight. 'I wonder,' mused Geoffrey Grigson in *Notes from an Odd Country*, 'if deity and art don't originate in sparkle, glitter, crystal, refracted light, an abstracted portion of sun, the gravel after rain . . .'

Jaccottet is an intensely visual poet. Nabokov, in *The Real Life of Sebastian Knight*, says of Clare Bishop that 'she possessed that real sense of beauty which has less to do with art than with the constant readiness to discern the halo round a frying-pan or the likeness between a weeping willow and a Skye terrier'; and so it is with Jaccottet. But the artist with whom he has the greatest affinity is Tal-Coat, whose characteristic manner, developed in the 1950s, has been called 'lyrical abstraction': a natural scene or object is teased out until precise subject-matter disappears and we are left with a few brush-strokes only, black on white, which qualify, so to speak, as ideograms — even as haiku, what Grigson calls 'a few words in space'.

Jaccottet too developed a mode of lyrical abstraction consciously based on oriental precedents. *Airs* is a book of very short poems which, says the author, *'raconte de façon cachée une histoire d'amour'* ('contains a hidden love story'). The love story is there certainly, but the most striking thing about the poems is their technique — a few brush-strokes only, a few words in space, in contrast to the traditional rhetoric of *L'Effraie* and *L'Ignorant*; and, few as the lines are, we have to read between them. What do we miss in this poetry? Several things: vitality sometimes, humour, the demotic, the abrasive surfaces of the modern world. It's sparsely populated, and there's a certain thinness of texture, albeit deliberate. Sometimes it seems refined out of existence. There is (almost) no *sea*; for this is an inland poetry of river and hill, the country road, the lake in the woods. People? One often makes out a Muse-like presence but, except for actual brief appearances, as in 'Glimpses', she remains a shadowy figure. Most cheat with their own experience, he says, 'put it between parentheses, make it vanish'; yet he implicitly concedes value — perhaps, paradoxically, the greatest value — to the art of which he represents himself as a 'self-effacing' practitioner:

> (*Nothing at all, a footfall on the road,
> yet more mysterious than guide or god.*)

He speaks of *'la goutte d'eau pur'* ('the pure water-drop') of poetry, contrasting it with the complex stream of discourse favoured by critical theory: 'Such nonsense to set up against such knowledge, ingenuity, doctrine! But perhaps poetry relies precisely on what is not argument. I, at least, rely on it.' The 'pure water-drop', visible in *Airs*, grows audible in *Pensées sous les nuages* ('Cloud Thoughts', 1983), a volume which moves from the photographic mode of 'Glimpses' to the celebratory music of 'To Henry Purcell'. Jaccottet's poems take place, characteristically, in

14

the absence of most other noise; but in the tentative birdsong, running water and rustling leaves of his landscape one hears an enchantment, what used to be called the music of the spheres:

If ever they speak above us
in the starry trees of their April.

Derek Mahon

'La nuit est une grande cité endormie'

La nuit est une grande cité endormie
où le vent souffle . . . Il est venu de loin jusqu'à
l'asile de ce lit. C'est la minuit de juin.
Tu dors, on m'a mené sur ces bords infinis,
le vent secoue le noisetier. Vient cet appel
qui se rapproche et se retire, on jurerait
une lueur fuyant à travers bois, ou bien
les ombres qui tournoient, dit-on, dans les enfers.
(Cet appel dans la nuit d'été, combien de choses
j'en pourrais dire, et de tes yeux . . .) Mais ce n'est que
l'oiseau nommé l'effraie, qui nous appelle au fond
de ces bois de banlieue. Et déjà notre odeur
est celle de la pourriture au petit jour,
déjà sous notre peau si chaude perce l'os,
tandis que sombrent les étoiles au coin des rues.

'The June night is like a city of the dead'

The June night is like a city of the dead
where the wind sighs, wind that has come
a long way to the shelter of our bed.
It shakes a hazel while you sleep
and I drift to the edge of a dream;
then I hear cries, nearby, far-off,
like fugitive lights in a forest
or shadows flickering in hell.
(So much to be said of those cries
and so much to be said of your eyes!)
It's only a bird, the screech owl,
in the thick of these urban woods;
but already our smell is the smell
of something rotten at dawn; already
bone pierces the living skin
while stars fade at the end of the street.

'Comme je suis un étranger dans notre vie'

Comme je suis un étranger dans notre vie,
je ne parle qu'à toi avec d'étranges mots,
parce que tu seras peut-être ma patrie,
mon printemps, nid de paille et de pluie aux rameaux,

ma ruche d'eau qui tremble à la pointe du jour,
ma naissante Douceur-dans-la-nuit . . . (Mais c'est l'heure
que les corps heureux s'enfouissent dans leur amour
avec des cris de joie, et une fille pleure

dans la cour froide. Et toi? Tu n'es pas dans la ville,
tu ne marches pas à la rencontre des nuits,
c'est l'heure où seul avec ces paroles faciles

je me souviens d'une bouche réelle . . .) Ô fruits
mûrs, source des chemins dorés, jardins de lierre,
je ne parle qu'à toi, mon absente, ma terre . . .

'Being a stranger in this life, I speak'

Being a stranger in this life, I speak
only to you, and in strange sentences,
since you may prove the familiar land I seek,
my spring, my dewy straw-nest in the branches,

my gush of water trembling at first light,
my budding Sweetness-in-the-Dark; but now,
while striving bodies dive to their delight
with cries of love, a lone girl whimpers low

in the cold yard. And you? You're out of reach,
not marching out tonight to face the town.
Lying alone here with my facile speech

I think of your real mouth . . . O ripening fruits
and ivied gardens, depths of golden lane,
I speak only to you, my absent roots.

'Je sais maintenant que je ne possède rien'

Je sais maintenant que je ne possède rien,
pas même ce bel or qui est feuilles pourries,
encore moins ces jours volant d'hier à demain
à grands coups d'ailes vers une heuereuse patrie.

Elle fut avec eux, l'émigrante fanée,
la beauté faible, avec ses secrets décevants,
vêtue de brume. On l'aura sans doute emmenée
ailleurs, par ces forêts pluvieuses. Comme avant,

je me retrouve au seuil d'un hiver irréel
où chante le bouvreuil obstiné, seul apel
qui ne cesse pas, comme le lierre. Mais qui peut dire

quel est son sens? Je vois ma santé se réduire,
pareille à ce feu bref au-devant du brouillard
qu'un vent glacial avive, efface . . . Il se fait tard.

'I know now I possess nothing of my own'

I know now I possess nothing of my own —
not even the gold of these dead leaves, still less
these days flying past into the unknown
beating their great wings toward what happy place.

The exhausted emigrant, she was there too,
a frail beauty with her mysterious lore
mist-clothed. No doubt they've taken her by now
elsewhere in these dripping forests. As before

I stand on the threshold of a wintry sky
listening to one fierce finch, its deathless cry
as obstinate as ivy. Who can translate

its meaning? Now my strength begins to fail
like the brief fire in the fog an icy gale
fans and extinguishes. It's getting late.

Portovenere

La mer est de nouveau obscure. Tu comprends,
c'est la dernière nuit. Mais qui vais-je appelant?
Hors l'écho, je ne parle à personne, à personne.
Où s'écroulent les rocs, la mer est noire, et tonne
dans sa cloche de pluie. Une chauve-souris
cogne aux barreaux de l'air d'un vol comme surpris,
tous ces jours sont perdus, déchirés par ses ailes
noires, la majesté de ces eaux trop fidèles
me laisse froid, puisque je ne parle toujours
ni à toi, ni à rien. Qu'ils sombrent, ces 'beaux jours'!
Je pars, je continue à vieillir, peu m'importe,
sur qui s'en va la mer saura claquer la porte.

Portovenere

The sea is dark again on my last night
but who or what am I calling upon tonight?
Aside from the echo there is nobody, nobody.
Beyond the crumbling rocks the iron-dark sea
booms in its bell of rain, and a bat flies
at the windows of the air in wild surprise.
My days, torn by its black wings, are in tatters;
the grandeur of these too-predictable waters
leaves me cold since I no longer know
how to communicate. Let the 'fine days' go!
I leave, an older man, what do I care,
the sea will slam its door on my departure.

Intérieur

Il y a longtemps que je cherche à vivre ici,
dans cette chambre que je fais semblant d'aimer,
la table, les objets sans soucis, la fenêtre
ouvrant au bout de chaque nuit d'autres verdures,
et le coeur du merle bat dans le lierre sombre,
partout des lueurs achèvent l'ombre vieillie.

J'accepte moi aussi de croire qu'il fait doux,
que je suis chez moi, que la journée sera bonne.
Il y a juste, au pied du lit, cette araignée
(à cause du jardin), je ne l'ai pas assez
piétinée, on dirait qu'elle travaille encore
au piège qui attend mon fragile fantôme . . .

Interior

I have been trying for a long time to live
here in this room I pretend to like
with its table, its thoughtless objects,
its window wide to the dawn leaves.
A blackbird throbs in the ivy; light
everywhere polishes off the ancient dark.

I would gladly believe the bad times are done,
that this is my home, that the sun will shine,
were it not for the spider in the dust
at the foot of the bed, strayed in from the garden.
I should have trampled it harder, you would think
it was still weaving a trap for my delicate ghost.

Les eaux et les forêts

1

La clarté de ces bois en mars est irréelle,
tout est encor si frais qu'à peine insiste-t-elle.
Les oiseaux ne sont pas nombreux; tout juste si,
très loin, où l'aubépine éclaire les taillis,
le coucou chante. On voit scintiller des fumées
qui emportent ce qu'on brûla d'une journée,
la feuille morte sert les vivantes couronnes,
et suivant la leçon des plus mauvais chemins,
sous les ronces, on rejoint le nid de l'anémone,
claire et commune comme l'étoile du matin.

2

Quand même je saurais le réseau de mes nerfs
aussi précaire que le toile d'araignée,
je n'en louerais pas moins ces merveilles de vert,
ces colonnes, même choisies pour la cognée,

et ces chevaux de bûcherons . . . Ma confiance
devrait s'étendre un jour à la hache, á l'éclair,
si la beauté de mars n'est que l'obéissance
du merle et de la violette, par temps clair.

3

Le dimanche peuple les bois d'enfants qui geignent,
de femmes vieillissantes; un garçon sur deux saigne
au genou, et l'on rentre avec des mouchoirs gris,
laissant de vieux papiers près de l'étang . . . Les cris
s'éloignent avec la lumière. Sous les charmes,
une fille tire sur sa jupe à chaque alarme,
l'air harassé. Toute douceur, celle de l'air
ou de l'amour, a la cruauté pour revers,
tout beau dimanche a sa rançon, comme les fêtes
ces taches sur les tables où le jour nous inquiète.

Streams and Forests

1

The brightness of these March woods is unreal,
everything still so fresh it hardly insists.
Not many birds yet; but where whitethorn
quickens the thickets a cuckoo sings,
and sparkling smoke carries away
whatever it was that was burnt today.
Dead leaves will make the living crown.
At the end of the shadiest paths,
among brambles, you will find an anemone
bright and ordinary like the morning star.

2

Even if I could examine the cobweb intricacies
of my nervous system, I would still
be able to praise these wooden
columns, even those chosen for destruction.

If the beauty of March consists in the obedience
of blackbird and violet to a clear sky,
I too must extend my confidence one day
to the lightning-flash of the axe.

3

Sunday fills the woods with complaining children,
ageing women, boys with bloody knees
and dirty handkerchiefs; and the pond
is littered with crumpled newspapers.
Shouts fade with the light; under the elms
a girl tugs resentfully at her skirt
if anyone passes. All gentleness, of the air
or of love, is harsh on the other side:
fine Sundays have their price, like parties
that leave wine-stains on the table at daybreak.

Toute autre inquiétude est encore futile,
je ne marcherai pas longtemps dans ces forêts,
et la parole n'est ni plus ni moins utile
que ces chatons de saule en terrain de marais :

peu importe qu'ils tombent en poussière s'ils brillent,
bien d'autres marcheront dans ces bois qui mourront,
peu importe que la beauté tombe pourrie,
puisqu'elle semble en la totale soumission.

All this anxiety is beside the point,
my walking in these woods will not be long,
and words are neither more nor less useful
than the willows rustling in the marshes.

Dust-destined, yes; but the dust glitters;
other mortals will walk here when I've gone.
As for the death of beauty, that hardly matters,
it shines forth in its very abdication.

Au petit jour

1

La nuit n'est pas ce que l'on croit, revers du feu,
chute du jour et négation de la lumière,
mais subterfuge fait pour nous ouvrir les yeux
sur ce qui reste irrévélé tant qu'on l'éclaire.

Les zélés serviteurs du visible éloignés,
sous le feuillage des ténèbres est établie
le demeure de la violette, le dernier
refuge de celui qui vieillit sans patrie . . .

2

Comme l'huile qui dort dans la lampe et bientôt
tout entière se change en lueur et respire
sous la lune emportée par le vol des oiseaux,
tu murmures et tu brûles. (Mais comment dire
cette chose qui est trop pure pour la voix?)
Tu es le feu naisssant sur les froides rivières,
l'alouette jaillie du champ . . . Je vois en toi
s'ouvrir et s'entêter la beauté de la terre.

3

Je te parle, mon petit jour. Mas tout cela
ne serait-il qu'un vol de paroles dans l'air?
Nomade est la lumière. Celle qu'on embrassa
devient celle qui fut embrassée, et se perd.
Qu'une dernière fois dans la voix qui l'implore
elle se lève donc et rayonne, l'aurore.

Daybreak

1

Night is not what we think, the reverse of fire,
sun-death and the negation of the light,
but a subterfuge intended to discover
whatever remains invisible in daylight.

The zealous servants of the visible
having withdrawn, the violet has made
its home now in the deepening shade,
the final refuge of the exiled soul.

2

Like the oil asleep in the lamp which suddenly,
beneath a moon swept by a flight of birds,
transforms itself to a glow and breathes,
you murmur and burn; and no voice
can convey the pure quality of it.
You are the light rising on cold rivers,
the lark sprung from the field;
the very earth is laid bare and elated.

3

I speak to you, daybreak, although all that I say
is only a flight of words in the air.
Light is fugitive, embrace it
and it becomes a shade; yet once
again, as if it had heard my prayer,
the sun rises and sends forth its first light.

La patience

Dans les cartes à jouer abattues sous la lampe
comme les papillons écroulés poussiéreux,
à travers le tapis de table et la fumée,
je vois ce qu'il vaut mieux ne voir pas affleurer
lorsque le tintement de l'heure dans les verres
annonce une nouvelle insomnie, la croissante
peur d'avoir peur dans le resserrement du temps,
l'usure du corps, l'éloignement des défenseurs.
Le vieil homme écarte les images passées
et, non sans réprimer un tremblement, regarde
la pluie glacée pousser la porte du jardin.

Patience

In the playing-cards spread out in the lamplight
like the powdery wings of fallen moths
I see beyond the smoke-wreathed tablecloths
something that would be better kept from sight —
a new insomnia the rung glasses chime,
fear of being afraid, contraction of time,
bodily attrition, collapse of resistance.
Old men discard their previous existence,
quelling a qualm, and turn to contemplate
the hailstones slashing at the garden gate.

La voix

Qui chante là quand toute voix se tait? Qui chante
avec cette voix sourde et pure un si beau chant?
Serait-ce hors de la ville, à Robinson, dans un
jardin couvert de neige? Ou est-ce là tout près,
quelqu'un qui ne se doutait pas qu'on l'écoutât?
Ne soyons pas impatients de la savoir
puisque le jour n'est pas autrement précédé
par l'invisible oiseau. Mais faisons seulement
silence. Une voix monte, et comme un vent de mars
aux bois vieillis porte leur force, elle nous vient
sans larmes, souriant plutôt devant la mort.
Qui chantait là quand notre lampe s'est éteinte?
Nul ne le sait. Mais seul peut entendre le coeur
qui ne cherche la possession ni la victoire.

The Voice

What is it that sings when the other voices are silent?
Whose is that pure, deaf voice, that sibilant song?
Is it down the road on a snow-covered lawn
or close at hand, unaware of an audience?
This is the mysterious first bird of dawn.
Do you hear the voice increase in volume
and, as a March wind quickens a creaking tree,
sing mildly to us without fear,
content in the fact of death? Do you hear?
What does it sing in the grey dawn? Nobody knows;
but the voice is audible only to those
whose hearts seek neither possession nor victory.

L'ignorant

Plus je vieillis et plus je croîs en ignorance,
plus j'ai vécu, moins je possède et moins je règne.
Tout ce que j'ai, c'est un espace tour à tour
enneigé ou brillant, mais jamais habité.
Où est le donateur, le guide, le gardien?
Je me tiens dans ma chambre et d'abord je me tais
(le silence entre en serviteur mettre un peu d'ordre),
et j'attends qu'un à un les mensonges s'écartent:
que reste-t-il? que reste-t-il à ce mourant
qui l'empêche si bien de mourir? Quelle force
le fait encor parler entre ses quatre murs?
Pourrais-je le savoir, moi l'ignare et l'inquiet?
Mais je l'entends vraiment qui parle, et sa parole
pénètre avec le jour, encore que bien vague:

'Comme le feu, l'amour n'établit sa clarté
que sur la faute et la beauté des bois en cendres . . .'

Ignorance

The older I grow the more ignorant I become,
the longer I live the less I possess or control.
All I have is a little space, snow-dark
or glittering, never inhabited.
Where is the giver, the guide, the guardian?
I sit in my room and am silent; silence
arrives like a servant to tidy things up
while I wait for the lies to disperse.
And what remains to this dying man
that so well prevents him from dying?
What does he find to say to the four walls?
I hear him talking still, and his words
come in with the dawn, imperfectly understood:

'Love, like fire, can only reveal its brightness
on the failure and the beauty of burnt wood.'

Les gitans

Il ya a un feu sous les arbres:
on l'entend qui parle bas
à la nation endormie
près des portes de la ville.

Si nous marchons en silence,
âmes de peu de durée
entre les sombres demeures,
c'est de crainte que tu meures,
murmure perpétuel
de la lumière cachée.

The Gipsies

There are fires under the trees —
you can hear the low voice of the tribe
on the fringes of cities.

If, short-lived souls that we are,
we pass silently
on the dark road tonight,
it is for fear you should die,
perpetual murmur
around the hidden light.

Sur les pas de la lune

M'étant penché en cette nuit à la fenêtre,
je vis que le monde était devenu léger
et qu'il n'y avait plus d'obstacles. Tout ce qui
nous retient dans le jour semblait plutôt devoir
me porter maintenant d'une ouverture à l'autre
à l'intérieur d'une demeure d'eau vers quelque chose
de très faible et de trés lumineux comme l'herbe:
j'allais entrer dans l'herbe sans aucune peur,
j'allais rendre grâce à la fraîcheur de la terre,
sur les pas de la lune je dis oui et je m'en fus . . .

In the Steps of the Moon

Leaning out of the window tonight
I saw that the world was without weight
and there were no more obstacles. All
that detains us by day appeared, moreover,
to take me through one door after another
in an abode of water, towards something
as frail and luminous as the grass
I was about to enter without fear,
giving thanks for the freshness of the earth.
In the steps of the moon I said yes and off I went.

Paroles dans l'air

L'air si clair dit: 'Je fus un temps votre maison,
puis viendront d'autres voyageurs à votre place,
et vous qui aimiez tant ce séjour, où irez-
vous? Je vois bien de la poussière sur la terre,
mais vous me regardiez, et vos yeux paraissaient
ne pas m'être inconnus; mais vous chantiez parfois,
est-ce donc tout? Vous parliez même à demi-voix
à quelqu'un qui était souvent ensommeillé,
vous lui disiez que la lumière de la terre
était trop pure pour ne pas avoir un sens
qui échappât de quelque manière à la mort,
vous vous imaginiez avancer dans ce sens,
et cependant je ne vous entends plus: qu'avez-
vous fait? Que va penser surtout votre compagne?'

Elle répond à travers ses heureuses larmes:
'Il s'est changé en cette ombre qui lui plaisait.'

Words in the Air

The clear air said: 'I was your home once
but other guests have taken your place;
where will you go who liked it here so much?
You looked at me through the thick dust
of the earth, and your eyes were known to me.
You sang sometimes, you even whispered low
to someone else who was often asleep,
you told her the light of the earth
was too pure not to point a direction
which somehow avoided death. You imagined
yourself advancing in that direction;
but now I no longer hear you. What have you done?
Above all, what is your lover going to think?'

And she, his friend, replied through tears of happiness:
'He has changed into the shade that pleased him best.'

Le locataire

Nous habitons une maison légère haut dans les airs,
le vent et la lumière la cloisonnent en se croisant,
parfois tout est si clair que nous en oublions les ans,
nous volons dans un ciel à chaque porte plus ouvert.

Les arbres sont en bas, l'herbe plus bas, le monde vert,
scintillant le matin et, quand vient la nuit, s'éteignant,
et les montagnes qui respirent dans l'éloignement
sont si minces que le regard errant passe au travers.

La lumière est bâtie sur un abîme, elle est tremblante,
hâtons-nous donc de demeurer dans ce vibrant séjour,
car elle s'enténèbre de poussière en peu de jours
ou bien elle se brise et tout à coup nous ensanglante.

Porte le locataire dans la terre, toi, servante!
Il a les yeux fermés, nous l'avons trouvé dans la cour,
si tu lui as donné entre deux portes ton amour,
descends-le maintenant dans l'humide maison des plantes.

The Tenant

We live in an airy house in the cloud kingdom
with wind and sun instead of ceilings and floors;
sometimes it is all so clear we forget the time
and fly in a heaven of ever more open doors.

There are trees down there, grass, a whole green world
glittering in the morning, extinguished at night;
as for the dozing mountains, fold upon fold,
the eye sees straight through them, they are so slight.

The light stands on a ravine and trembles there —
be quick, then, to inhabit this vibrant hut
for it will darken with dust in a month or a year
and cave in, covering us with blood and soot.

Bury the tenant in the earth, maidservant, lover:
his eyes are closed, we found him in the yard.
Having nursed him from the one door to the other,
now lay him out in his moist leguminous bed.

Que la fin nous illumine

Sombre ennemi qui nous combats et nous resserres,
laisse-moi, dans le peu de jours que je détiens,
vouer ma faiblesse et ma force à la lumière:
et que je sois changé en éclair à la fin.

Moins il y a d'avidité et de faconde
en nos propos, mieux on les néglige pour voir
jusque dans leur hésitation briller le monde
entre le matin ivre et la légèreté du soir.

Moins nos larmes apparaîtront brouillant nos yeux
et nos personnes par la crainte garrottées,
plus les regards iront s'éclaircissant et mieux
les égarés verront les portes enterrées.

L'effacement soit ma façon de resplendir,
la pauvreté surcharge de fruits notre table,
la mort, prochaine ou vague selon son désir,
soit l'aliment de la lumière inépuisable.

That the End Enlighten Us

Dark enemy, you who brace us in the fight,
let me, in the few days still left to spend,
devote my strength and weakness to the light
and so be changed to lightning in the end.

The gabbling mouths and animated eyes
grow easier to ignore even as they work;
the world gleams in their very hesitancies
between high morning and light-headed dark.

If we could stop whining and overcome
the fear that strangles us, behind, before,
our vision might improve, the lost become
more confident in their search for the buried door.

Let self-effacement be my way of blazing
and poverty weigh our table down with fruit;
death, far or near according to its choosing,
sustain, as ever, the inexhaustible light.

Dans un tourbillon de neige

Ils chevauchent encore dans les espaces glacés,
les quelques cavaliers que la mort n'a pas pu lasser.

Ils allument des feux dans la neige de loin en loin,
à chaque coup de vent il en flambe au moins un de moins.

Ils sont incroyablement petits, sombres, pressés,
devant l'immense, blanc et lent malheur à terrasser.

Certes, ils n'amassent plus dans leurs greniers ni or ni foin,
mais y cachant l'espoir fourbi avec le plus grand soin.

Ils courent les chemins par le pesant monstre effacés,
peut-être se font-ils si petits pour le mieux chasser?

Finalement, c'est bien toujours avec le même poing
qu'on se défend contre le souffle de l'immonde groin.

During a Snowstorm

I see them ride still in the icy places,
those few horsemen death never reduces.

They light fires here and there in the snow,
fires that go out whenever the winds blow.

Such tiny figures, desperate and dark
before the great white adversary they seek.

Their lofts, of course, hold neither gold nor grain,
merely the bright hope polished with such pain.

They pursue trails erased by the monster's size,
having grown small to take it by surprise.

In the end we always make use of the same fist
to fight off the bad breath of the foul beast.

Les distances

Tournent les martinets dans les hauteurs de l'air:
plus haut encore tournent les astres invisibles.
Que le jour se retire aux extrémités de la terre,
apparaîtront ces feux sur l'étendue de sombre sable . . .

Ainsi nous habitons un domaine de mouvements
et de distances; ainsi le coeur
va de l'arbre à l'oiseau, de l'oiseau aux astres lointains,
de l'astre à son amour. Ainsi l'amour
dans la maison fermée s'accroît, tourne et travaille,
serviteur des soucieux portant une lampe à la main.

Distances

Swifts turn in the heights of the air;
higher still turn the invisible stars.
When day withdraws to the ends of the earth
their fires shine on a dark expanse of sand.

We live in a world of motion and distance.
The heart flies from tree to bird,
from bird to distant star,
from star to love; and love grows
in the quiet house, turning and working,
servant of thought, a lamp held in one hand.

Fin d'hiver

Peu de chose, rien qui chasse
l'effroi de perdre l'espace
est laissé à l'âme errante

Mais peut-être, plus légère,
incertaine qu'elle dure,
est-elle celle qui chante
avec la voix la plus pure
les distances de la terre

'Une semaison de larmes'

Une semaison de larmes
sur le visage changé,
la scintillante saison
des rivières dérangées:
chagrin qui creuse la terre

L'âge regarde la neige
s'éloigner sur les montagnes

End of Winter

Not much, nothing to dispel
the fear of wasting space
is left the itinerant soul

Except perhaps a voice
unconfident and light,
uncertainly put forth,
with which to celebrate
the reaches of the earth

'A dispersion of tears'

A dispersion of tears
on the changed face,
the glittering season
of rivers in spate,
grief scoring the earth

Age watches snow recede
from the mountain peaks

'Dans l'herbe à l'hiver survivant'

Dans l'herbe à l'hiver survivant
ces ombres moins pesantes qu'elle,
des timides bois patients
sont la discrète, la fidèle,

l'encore imperceptible mort

Toujours dans le jour tournant
ce vol autour de nos corps
Toujours dans le champ du jour
ces tombes d'ardoise bleue

Lune à l'aube d'été

Dans l'air de plus en plus clair
scintille encore cette larme
ou faible flamme dans du verre
quand du sommeil des montagnes
monte une vapeur dorée

Demeure ainsi suspendue
sur la balance de l'aube
entre la braise promise
et cette perle perdue

'These wood-shadows, timid, patient'

These wood-shadows, timid, patient,
lighter even than the grass
that survived the winter,
are the discreet, faithful,

barely perceptible shadows of death

Always in the daytime
circling our bodies
Always in the open field
these tombstones of blue slate

Dawn Moon

Through ever clearer air
there gleams still this tear,
a windowed candle-flame,
when from the sleep of mountains
rises a golden steam

Retain your balance there
in the summer dawn,
half promised ember
half disregarded pearl

'Dans l'enceinte du bois d'hiver'

Dans l'enceinte du bois d'hiver
sans entrer tu peux t'emparer
de l'unique lumière due:
elle n'est pas ardent bûcher
ni lampe aux branches suspendue

Elle est le jour sur l'écorce
l'amour qui se dissémine
peut-être la clarté divine
à qui la hache donne force

'Toute fleur n'est que de la nuit'

Toute fleur n'est que de la nuit
qui feint de s'être rapprochée

Mais là d'où son parfum s'élève
je ne puis espérer entrer
c'est pourquoi tant il me trouble
et me fait si longtemps veiller
devant cette porte fermée

Toute couleur, toute vie
naît d'où le regard s'arrête

Ce monde n'est que la crête
d'un invisible incendie

'Without entering you can seize'

Without entering you can seize
the unique light locked
in the winter woods:
no bonfire this,
no lamp hung in the branches

But daybreak on the bark,
the love that fertilizes,
perhaps the holy light
an axe-flash emphasizes

'Each flower is a little night'

Each flower is a little night
pretending to draw near

But where its scent rises
I cannot hope to enter
which is why it bothers me
so much and why I sit so long
before this closed door

Each colour, each incarnation
begins where the eyes stop

This world is merely the tip
of an unseen conflagration

Martinets

Au moment orageux du jour
au moment hagard de la vie
ces faucilles au ras de la paille

Tout crie soudain plus haut
que ne peut gravir l'ouïe

❧

'Il y aura toujours dans mon oeil cependant'

Il y aura toujours dans mon oeil cependant
une invisible rose de regret
comme quand au-dessus d'un lac
a passé l'ombre d'un oiseau

❧

'Monde né d'une déchirure'

Monde né d'une déchirure
apparu pour être fumée!

Néanmoins la lampe allumée
sur l'interminable lecture

❧

Swifts

At the stormy moment of dawn
at the apprehensive time
these sickles in the corn

Everything suddenly cries higher
than any ear can climb

∽

'Meanwhile my eye will retain'

Meanwhile my eye will retain
an invisible rose of regret
as when a bird-shadow
passes over a lake

∽

'World born of a lesion'

World born of a lesion
and destined to be smoke

Even so the lamplight
on an unfinishable book

∽

'Raisins et figues'

Raisins et figues
couvés au loin par les montagnes
sous les lents nuages
et la fraîcheur:
sans doute, sans doute . . .

Vient un moment où l'aîné se couche
presque sans force. On voit
de jour en jour
son pas moins assuré.

Il ne s'agit plus de passer
comme l'eau entre les herbes:
cela ne se tourne pas.

Lorsque le maître lui-même
si vite est emmené si loin,
je cherche ce qui peut le suivre:

ni la lanterne des fruits,
ni l'oiseau aventureux,
ni la plus pure des images;

plutôt le linge et l'eau changés,
la main qui veille,
plutôt le coeur endurant.

'Grapes and figs'

Grapes and figs
born far off in the mountains
under the slow clouds
and the fresh air —
oh yes, oh yes . . .

But there comes a time
when the eldest, tired,
retires early; from day to day
his step grows less assured.

No longer a question
of moving about
like water between its banks;
and this won't improve.

When the master himself
is taken so far so quickly
I look for what may follow —

not a lamp of fruit,
a fearless bird,
the purest of images,

but water and clean linen,
the loving hand
and the obstinate heart.

'Entre la plus lointaine étoile et nous'

Entre la plus lointaine étoile et nous,
la distance, inimaginable, reste encore
comme une ligne, un lien, comme un chemin.
S'il est un lieu hors de toute distance,
ce devait être là qu'il se perdait:
non pas plus loin de toute étoile, ni moins loin,
mais déjà presque dans un autre espace,
en dehors, entraîné hors des mesures.
Notre mètre, de lui à nous, n'avait plus cours:
autant, comme une lame, le briser sur le genou.

'Between us and the farthest star'

Between us and the farthest star
lie the unthinkable distances —
lines, tracks, paths. If there
is a place beyond this space
it would be there he disappeared;
neither farther nor less far
but in another space, abstracted
beyond measure. The ruler laid
from us to him lost continuity
like a sword broken across the knee.

'S'il se pouvait (qui saura jamais rien?)'

S'il se pouvait (qui saura jamais rien?)
qu'il ait encore un espèce d'être aujourd'hui,
de conscience même que l'on croirait proche,
serait-ce donc ici qu'il se tiendrait,
dans cet enclos, non pas dans la prairie?
Se pourrait-il qu'il attendît ici
comme à un rendez-vous donné 'près de la pierre',
qu'il eut l'emploi de nos pas muets, de nos larmes?
Comment savoir? Un jour ou l'autre, on voit
ces pierres s'enfoncer dans les herbes éternelles,
tôt ou tard il n'y a plus d'hôtes à convier
au repère à son tour enfoui,
plus même d'ombres dans nulle ombre.

'If it should be, and who can ever be sure'

If it should be, and who can ever be sure,
that he still has some kind of existence today,
of consciousness even, not too far away,
would it be here that he would stay,
in the garden rather than out in the pasture?
Might he be waiting there, as if
by arrangement, 'beside the stone'?
Might he have need of our voices, our tears?
I don't know; but one day or another will see
these stones buried by the eternal grass,
sooner or later there will be no one left
to visit the grave, which will be buried too,
not even shadows in that shadowless place.

'Chose brève, le temps de quelques pas dehors'

(Chose brève, le temps de quelques pas dehors,
mais plus étrange encor que les mages et les dieux.)

'Nothing at all, a footfall on the road'

(Nothing at all, a footfall on the road,
yet more mysterious than guide or god.)

On voit

On voit les écoliers courir à grands cris
dans l'herbe épaisse du préau.

Les hauts arbres tranquilles
et la lumière de dix heures en septembre
comme une fraîche cascade
les abritent encore de l'énorme enclume
qui étincelle d'étoiles par-delà.

*

L'âme, si frileuse, si farouche,
devra-t-elle vraiment marcher sans fin sur ce glacier,
seule, pieds nus, ne sachant plus même épeler
sa prière d'enfance,
sans fin punie de sa froideur par ce froid?

*

Elle s'approche du miroir rond
comme une bouche d'enfant
qui ne sait pas mentir,
vêtue d'une robe de chambre bleue
qui s'use elle aussi.

Cheveux bientôt couleur de cendre
sous le très lent feu du temps.

Le soleil du petit matin
fortifie encore son ombre.

*

Glimpses

The children run shouting
in the thick grass of the playground.

The tall tranquil trees
and the torrential light
of a September morning
protect them still from the anvil
sparkling with stars up there.

                    *

The soul, so chilly, so fierce, must it really
trudge up this glacier for ever,
solitary, in bare feet, no longer
remembering even its childhood prayer,
its coldness for ever punished by this cold?

                    *

Wrapped in a blue bath-robe
which is wearing out too,
she goes to a mirror round
like the mouth of a child
who doesn't know how to lie.

Hair the colour of ash now
in the slow burn of time;

and yet the morning sun
quickens her shadow still.

                    *

Derrière la fenêtre dont on a blanchi le cadre
(contre les mouches, contre les fantômes),
une tête chenue de vieil homme se penche
sur une lettre, ou les nouvelles du pays.
Le lierre sombre croît contre le mur.

Gardez-le, lierre et chaux, du vent de l'aube,
des nuits trop longues et de l'autre, éternelle.

At the window with its freshly whitewashed frame
(to keep out flies, to keep out ghosts)
the white head of an old man leans
over a letter or the local news.
Against the wall dark ivy grows.

Save him, ivy and lime, from the dawn wind,
from long nights and the other, eternal night.

Le mot joie

Je suis comme quelq'un qui creuse dans la brume
à la recherche de ce qui échappe à la brume
pour avoir entendu un peu plus loin des pas
et des paroles entre des passants échangées . . .

＊

L'aurais-je donc inventé, le pinceau du couchant
sur la toile rugueuse de la terre,
l'huile dorée du soir sur les prairies et sur les bois?
C'était pourtant comme la lampe sur la table avec le pain.

＊

Mais chaque jour, peut-être, on peut reprendre
le filet déchiré, maille après maille,
et ce serait, dans l'espace plus haut,
comme recoudre, astre à astre, la nuit . . .

＊

Comme on voit maintenant dans les jardins de février
brûler ces petits feux de feuilles
(et l'on dirait que c'est moins pour nettoyer
le clos que pour aider la lumière à s'élargir),
est-il bien vrai que nous ne pouvons plus
en faire autant, avec notre coeur invisible?

＊

Qu'on me le montre, celui qui aurait conquis la certitude
et qui rayonnerait à partir de là dans la paix
comme une montagne qui s'éteint la dernière
et ne frémit jamais sous la pesée de la nuit.

The Word Joy

I am searching here in the fog
for something escaped from the fog
having heard steps in the distance
and the voices of passers-by.

*

Perhaps I imagined it, the sunset brush
on the rough canvas of earth,
a golden evening oil
on fields and woods; but it looked
like lamplit bread on a kitchen table.

*

Each day, perhaps, you might replace
the stitches in the severed net —
thus, in the distances of space,
to sew up, star by star, the night.

*

These bonfires in the February gardens
lit less for tidiness, you would say,
than to help spread the light,
can we ourselves manage no more
than this with our secret heart?

*

Show me the man who has found certitude
and shines in peace like the last
peak to fade at twilight, never
wincing under the weight of night.

À Henry Purcell

Écoute: comment se peut-il
que notre voix troublée se mêle ainsi
aux étoiles?

Il lui a fait gravir le ciel
sur des degrés de verre
par la grâce juvénile de son art.

*

Il nous a fait entendre le passage des brebis
qui se pressent dans la poussière de l'été céleste
et dont nous n'avons jamais bu le lait.

Il les a rassemblées dans la bergerie nocturne
où de la paille brille entre les pierres.
La barrière sonore est refermée:
fraîcheur de ces paisibles herbes à jamais.

*

Songe à ce que serait pour ton ouïe,
toi qui es à l'écoute de la nuit,
une très lente neige
de cristal.

*

On imagine une comète
qui reviendrait après des siècles
du royaume des morts
et, cette nuit, traverserait le nôtre
en y semant les mêmes graines . . .

*

To Henry Purcell

Listen: how is it
that our troubled voice mingles like this
with the stars?

He has scaled the heavens
on rungs of glass
by the youthful grace of his art.

*

We hear the passing of ewes
who throng the dust of the celestial summer,
whose milk we have never drunk.

He has herded them into the fold of night
where straw shines among the stones,
and the gate bangs shut.
The coolness of these quiet grasses for ever . . .

*

What do we hear
who tune in to the night?
A leisurely snow
of crystal.

*

Imagine a comet
returning centuries hence
from the kingdom of the dead,
crossing our century tonight
and sowing the same seeds . . .

*

Pendant que j'écoute,
le reflet d'une bougie
tremble dans le miroir
comme une flamme tressée
à de l'eau.

Cette voix aussi, n'est-elle pas l'écho
d'une autre, plus réelle?
Va-t-il l'entendre, celui qui se débat
entre les mains toujours trop lentes
du bourreau?
L'entendrai-je, moi?

Si jamais ils parlent au-dessus de nous
entre les arbres constellés de leur avril.

*

Tu es assis
devant le métier haut dressé de cette harpe.

Même invisible, je t'ai reconnu,
tisserand des ruisseaux surnaturels.

While I listen
the reflection of a candle
flickers in the mirror
like a flame woven
of water.

Might not this voice be the echo
of another, more real?
And will that ever be heard
by those thrashing in terror?
Will I hear it myself?

If ever they speak above us
in the starry trees of their April.

*

You are seated before
the tense loom of the harp.

I know you, though invisible,
weaver of supernatural streams.

Acknowledgements

The following translations appeared first in *Philippe Jaccottet: Selected Poems*, translated and introduced by Derek Mahon and published by Viking/Penguin in 1987. Special thanks are due to Paul Keegan.

The poems by Philippe Jaccottet appeared originally in the following collections published by Éditions Gallimard: *L'Effraie*, 1953 (pages 16–28); *L'Ignorant*, 1957 (30–50); *Airs*, 1967 (52–58); *Leçons*, 1969 (60–64); *À la lumière d'hiver*, 1977 (page 66) and *Pensées sous les nuages*, 1983 (68–76).

Acknowledgement is due to Bloodaxe Books for permission to reprint two poems from *Pensées sous les nuages*.